ALSC PROGRAM
SUPPORT
PUBLICATIONS

Programming for Outreach Services to Children

Association for Library Service to Children

Prepared by
Jane Lenser

Evelyn Walker
Series Editor

American Library Association
Chicago and London 1994

Cover design by Richmond Jones

Text design by Dianne M. Rooney

Acquisitions editor: Bonnie J. Smothers

Managing editor: Bruce Frausto

Composition by ALA Production Services in Times Roman using Ventura Publisher 4.2

Printed on 50-pound Finch Opaque, a pH-neutral stock, and bound in 90-pound Scott Index by IPC, St. Joseph, Michigan

The paper used in this publication meets the minimum requirements of American National Standard for Information Sciences —Permanence of Paper for Printed Library Materials, ANSI Z39.48-1984. ∞

Copyright © 1994 by the American Library Association. All rights reserved except those which may be granted by Sections 107 and 108 of the Copyright Revision Act of 1976.

Printed in the United States of America.

98 97 96 95 94   5 4 3 2 1

Contents

Criteria 2
Possible Outreach Program Sites 3
Checklist for Program Planning 5
Conclusion 9
Suggested Resources and Aids 9

Programming for Outreach Services to Children

Public libraries have traditionally offered children and their families a variety of programs held at the library. These programs are important and fill a definite need, but alone they are not sufficient to reach the maximum possible number of people. Every public library has a percentage of non-users. Many may be intimidated by institutions such as libraries as well as the librarians who work there. This group often is composed of minorities, the poor, the uneducated, or non-English-speaking populations. We must reach out to nonusers and introduce them to the benefits of the library's materials and services. Eventually, some may be persuaded to visit the library and become loyal patrons.

Other problems often limit people who would otherwise frequent the library. A lack of transportation can cause difficulty. Public transportation may be available in urban areas, but in most rural or suburban communities, it is inadequate or nonexistent. Public libraries often extend an open invitation to school classes to visit for a program. Teachers may have good intentions to take advantage of these offers but are frequently hindered by transportation costs, discipline problems, lack of parent chaperones, and tight class scheduling.

The tradition of library outreach is rich in innovative ways of bringing library services to people. Ever since Margaret Edwards packed up her horse-drawn book wagon and rode around the slums of Baltimore, librarians have known that in order to successfully reach much of our population, we must take our show on the road and offer programs at sites other than the library building.

Successful outreach programming requires careful thought and planning. The following list can help get the plans under way.

Criteria

1. Determine the purpose and scope of the outreach program you are planning. Set goals you hope to achieve.
2. Research the community to determine what programs, if any, are already being offered to your audience. Avoid duplication.
3. Seek the support of the library administration and all library departments that may be directly or indirectly involved in the outreach program.
4. Educate staff about customs and lifestyle differences in other cultures. Sensitivity training can be very valuable for all involved. Remember to train any new staff members who are hired after the initial training takes place.
5. Involve community agencies that may be serving your audience's needs in other ways. Enlist their assistance and keep them informed. They can also be very valuable in getting the word out to the appropriate people.
6. Consider the needs and characteristics of the age level targeted. Plan the content, materials, structure, and program length accordingly.
7. Involve the parents whose children may be interested in the program. Often they will come with their children, so take advantage of the situation. Ask them to help or take along a bag of paperbacks and magazines for them to read during the program.
8. If there is a contact person at the site of the outreach program, gain his or her support. If you do not speak the language of the audience, get an interpreter who supports your efforts. Enlist a bilingual program teacher to inter-

pret or supply you with other possible resources. The foreign-language department of your local community college can also be a great resource for interpreters. Inquire about students in need of intern projects, and post announcements on the departmental bulletin board. It is also helpful if the prospective audience knows and respects the interpreter.
9. Evaluate the success of the program. Note what went well and what you would do differently next time.

Possible Outreach Program Sites

Indoor

The sky is the limit! Organize a baseball card swap, share a puppet story, do booktalks, make a holiday craft, hold a film festival, or read some favorite books. Following are a few suggestions for planning your creative programs.

The Bloomingdale Public Library in Bloomingdale, Illinois, has participated in a storytelling festival at the Stratford Square Mall for many years. Director Mary Rodne shared some tips learned from experience.

To arrange a storytelling festival or other program in a shopping mall, contact the person in charge of promotions in the mall's office. Malls may have strict guidelines that must be followed such as that programs must continue to be presented until the mall closes or that only signage made by the mall's promotion department is allowed.

It is advantageous to request placement in a high-traffic area to attract the largest audience. Storytellers dressed in costumes receive the most attention and are more easily approached by passersby.

A portable sound system is a must for shopping mall programs. Mall acoustics are often very poor, and you will be competing with background noise from people and possibly a bubbling fountain or splashing waterfall!

When the "Together is Better... Let's Read" reading materials from the American Library Association and McDonald's restaurants arrived at the Arlington Heights Memorial Library in Arlington Heights, Illinois, they sparked the idea of holding storytimes at a local McDonald's.

In a joint effort between the Youth Services and Community Services Departments, twenty-minute storytimes were held for nine weeks at a McDonald's restaurant near the library. The restaurant management was very cooperative and even invited staff from other McDonald's locations to observe the innovative programs.

Judy Moskal, Program Coordinator for Youth Services, recommends choosing the location within the restaurant very carefully. Avoid the ordering area, block off the indoor playground if there is one, and position yourself so that latecomers can easily join in without causing a major disruption.

Mid-morning is a good time for the program. It is a fairly quiet time for McDonald's, and many families may stay after the storytime to have lunch.

Selecting materials to share takes some careful planning. Choose materials that are large, eye-catching, snappy, and upbeat. The Arlington Heights Memorial Library staff wanted their stories to be inviting enough so that children arriving in the middle of the storytime could quickly feel a part of the group.

Again, expect background noise, so bring a sound system if possible.

Schools offer a variety of possibilities for programs. Visit individual classes or grades, or present an assembly for the entire school. School open houses are a great place to give out library information and do storytelling. Visit high school child-care classes to discuss sharing books with children and storytelling techniques. Attend a faculty meeting or institute day, or visit a PTA or other parent group meeting to discuss choosing books for children or gift ideas for different ages. Schools are also the natural location for promoting library summer reading programs.

Attend scout meetings and introduce library materials

containing information that will help scouts earn a particular badge. Repeat successful in-library programs that the group would enjoy.

Contact a prison or correctional center in your area to arrange to present stories or movies to the children of prisoners during long visiting hours.

Other possible indoor sites are preschools and daycare homes, housing projects, YMCAs and YWCAs, churches and synagogues, hospitals, homes of homebound children, the Salvation Army, and homeless shelters or centers for abused women and children.

Outdoor

Have a pet show, teach a messy craft, hold a battle of the bands for young adults, teach and play outdoor games, or make kites and have a kite-flying contest.

Hold programs in parks, playgrounds, vacant lots, the sidewalk in front of shopping centers, community festivals or fairs, bookmobile stops, or the front steps of apartment buildings.

Checklist for Program Planning

Personnel

One staff member should be in charge of a program, although much work can be delegated to others. Recruit volunteers or older students to assist with making name tags or other preparations. Consider staff talents and interests when assigning duties. When using audio-visual equipment, it is a definite advantage to have a staff member available who can troubleshoot problems.

Space/Facilities

Visit the site of the program ahead of time, if possible. Take note of any pertinent details such as the location of electrical outlets, coat racks, rest rooms, dressing rooms, and exits.

Also be aware of the room's ventilation, temperature, and lighting, and ask about modifying them if they are unsatisfactory. Check out the facility's accessibility to wheelchairs and strollers. Listen during your visit to determine if you are likely to be competing with noise from traffic, trains, or airplanes, or other distracting noises.

If it is impractical to visit the site prior to the program, at least arrive early so that any snags can be worked out before the program is scheduled to begin. Verify details via phone with the contact person at the site to ensure that the facility will meet your needs.

In cases where the facility will be providing equipment, such as a video recorder and television or sound system, get acquainted with the operations in advance. Check on the placement of tables, chairs, or anything else required of the facility.

Costs

Funding for outreach programs is usually included in the general programming budget. Mileage for the staff running the program will be an extra cost for which to budget. Outreach programs are often so innovative that costs can be covered by grants or donations from businesses or community organizations. Program costs can be shared with the institution housing the program.

Programs can be inexpensive to hold. Booktalks, films, and repeats of staff-led programs at the library cost little other than staff time. With a little research, library staff can easily lead a workshop on beginning sign language, babysitting, or many other topics that will result in a worthwhile program with a minimal cost. There are many sources and alternatives to explore if funding is a problem.

Time/Schedule

When scheduling programs out of the library, do your homework ahead of time. Find out what time students get home from school, when scouts or other regular activities in which they may be involved are held, and what they do during the summer. If possible, offer a program at a variety of times

(e.g., after school, evenings, and Saturdays) to discover the audience's preference.
 The amount of staff time required is another consideration of scheduling. Planning for an outreach program can take a lot longer than planning for an in-house program. Travel time to and from the site must also be planned for. Evaluate the staff workload when determining the number and frequency of the programs.

Registration

Advance registration for a program has several important benefits. If a program requires supplies, knowing the number of people planning to attend will ensure that you have enough but will prevent buying too many. If a registered program fills to its capacity quickly, additional sessions can be added to meet the demand. If few people sign up for a program, you may wish to cancel it or combine two sessions if both have low registrations. Often a large turnout is not a major problem as long as it does not come as a surprise. A bigger room can be secured and more chairs can be set up ahead of time. Advance registration also gives you the opportunity to speak to each participant, answer questions, and pass on any appropriate reminders.
 If an outreach program is aimed at non–English-speaking populations or other groups who may be intimidated by the public library, explore alternatives to requiring that they visit or call the library to register. Otherwise, the benefit of holding the program at an alternate site where the audience feels more comfortable will be diminished. If there is a contact person at the site, perhaps he or she can tally the reservations for you.
 For programs conducted on a drop-in basis, it may be advantageous to have participants or their parents sign in. The list can then be used as a mailing list or as a means of discovering who is being reached and who is not.

Publicity/Public Relations

Publicizing outreach programs requires more creativity than doing so for regular in-library programs. Seek the support of local schools, community centers, and churches in the area you wish to target. Teachers and other neighborhood leaders can be invaluable in helping get the word out to the appropriate audience. Visit the neighborhood and distribute flyers to people. Enlist volunteers or neighborhood residents to assist, especially if they speak the native language of the area and you do not. Provide local newspapers with a press release and request a photographer for programs of special interest.

If possible, bring related books and audiovisual materials to the program and let patrons check them out. Paperback books are much less bulky and cheaper to replace than hardcover books if loss or damage occurs. Remember to bring materials needed for checkout, such as pens, lists, or date cards. Allow extra time for browsing and checking out before and after the program. Instituting off-site checkouts will take some good cooperation on the part of the circulation staff. Do your best to overcome any staff objections. If you are unable to check materials out to participants, compile a list of related titles that are available at the library. For booktalks or storytimes, also supply library staff with a list of materials used in case a patron comes to the library later looking for one of the books and is unsure of the title.

Evaluation

One of the most effective ways of gauging a program's popularity is by watching the audience react during the presentation. Children are especially open with their emotions, both good and bad. Another way is to talk to participants informally following the program. Older children and parents can fill out an evaluation form if language or illiteracy is not a problem.

Evaluate the cost per participant, and also take into consideration the total staff time spent planning, traveling to and from, and conducting each program. Evaluate your program as soon as possible following the event, while details are fresh. A well-thought-out evaluation can be very helpful in planning future events and increasing their success.

9

Conclusion

The best advice for outreach programmers is to be flexible and keep their sense of humor. Even the most organized program can be interrupted by a fire alarm in a school or an open fire hydrant on the block during an outdoor summer storytime. There is little question that programming at alternate sites takes more time in planning, scheduling, and publicizing than in-library programs. Then why subject yourself to the extra hassle? The answer is that outreach programming is very rewarding. Being able to reach out to children and their families who would otherwise be unable to take part in library programs is definitely worth the effort.

Suggested Resources and Aids

Allen, Adela Artola. *Library Services for Hispanic Children: A Guide for Public and School Librarians.* Phoenix, Ariz.: Oryx Press, 1987.

Carlson, Pam. "Shining STARS: Public Library Service to Children in Shelters." *School Library Journal* 38 (July 1992): 18–21.

Edwards, Margaret A. *The Fair Garden and the Swarm of Beasts.* New York: Hawthorn Books, 1974.

Fish, James. "Responding to Cultural Diversity: A Library in Transition." *Wilson Library Bulletin* 66 (Feb. 1992): 34–38.

Hayden, Carla D., ed. *Venture into Cultures: A Resource Book of Multi-cultural Materials and Programs.* Chicago: American Library Assn., 1992.

Hoffert, Barbara. "Se Lea Español Aqui!" *Library Journal* 117 (July 1992): 34–37.

Naismith, Rachael. "Library Service to Migrant Farm Workers." *Library Journal* 114 (Mar. 1, 1989): 54–57.

10

Nauratil, Marcia J. *Public Libraries and Nontraditional Clienteles: The Politics of Special Services.* Westport, Conn.: Greenwood Press, 1985.

Nespeca, Sue McCleaf. "Reaching the Unserved: Libraries Can Attack Illiteracy." *School Library Journal* 36 (July 1990): 20–22.

Quezada, Shelley. "Mainstreaming Library Services to Multicultural Populations: The Evolving Tapestry." *Wilson Library Bulletin* 66 (Feb. 1992): 34–37.

Robotham, John S., and Lydia LaFleur. *Library Programs: How to Select, Plan and Produce Them.* 2d ed. Metuchen, N.J.: Scarecrow Press, 1981.

Saccardi, Marianne. "Books to Go: A Portable Reading Project." *School Library Journal* 35 (Sept. 1989): 168–72.

Jane Lenser has been doing programs for children both in the library and at outreach sites for over ten years. She began her library career as head librarian (and sole employee) of the Winnebago (Illinois) Public Library, a tiny storefront facility. Currently Lenser is the program coordinator of the Young People's Services Department of the Indian Trails Public Library in Wheeling, Illinois.